Pembrokeshire
Tea Shop Walks

Text: *Dennis Kelsall*
Series editor: *Tony Bowerman*
Photographs: *Dennis and Jan Kelsall, Alf Alderson, © Crown copyright (2017) Visit Wales, Adobe Stock, Dreamstime, Shutterstock, Nathan Walton, Glasshouse Café, National Trust/Colby Gardens*

Design: *Carl Rogers*

Northern Eye Books

Northern Eye Books

ISBN 978-1-908632-48-7

A CIP catalogue record for this book is available from the British Library.

www.northerneyebooks.co.uk

Cover: *Quayside tearooms, Lawrenny (Walk 7)*

Important Advice: The routes described in this book are undertaken at the reader's own risk. Walkers should take into account their level of fitness, wear suitable footwear and clothing, and carry food and water. It is also advisable to take the relevant OS map with you in case you get lost and leave the area covered by our maps.

Whilst every care has been taken to ensure the accuracy of the route directions, the publisher cannot accept responsibility for errors or omissions, or for changes in the details given. Nor can the publisher and copyright owners accept responsibility for any consequences arising from the use of this book.

If you find any inaccuracies in either the text or maps, please either write to us or email us at the addresses below. Thank you.

This edition published in 2017 by:
Northern Eye Books Limited
Northern Eye Books, Tattenhall, Cheshire CH3 9P
Email: tony@northerneyebooks.com

For sales enquiries, please call: 01928 723 744

www.walescoastpath.co.uk
www.top10walks.co.uk

Twitter: @Northerneyeboo
@Top10walks
@WalesCoastUK

Printed & bound in the UK by: Ashford Colour Press

Contents

The Land's End of Wales 4

Top 10 Walks: Tea Shop walks 6

1. **The Glasshouse Café**, Cilgerran 8

2. **Plumvanilla Café**, Narberth 14

3. **The Sound Café**, St David's 20

4. **The Boathouse Café**, Dale 26

5. **Garden Tearoom,** St Ishmael's 32

6. **Wavecrest Café**, Angle 38

7. **Quayside Tearooms**, Lawrenny 42

8. **Beach Break tearooms**, Manorbier. 46

9. **Caffè Vista**, Tenby 52

10. **Bothy Tearoom**, Colby Garden 58

Useful Information 64

The Land's End of Wales

Pembrokeshire is blessed with almost 200 miles of stunning coastline, a craggy peninsula that reaches out to the wild Atlantic Ocean. The seaward rim is a wavering line of haunting beauty and perpetual contrast; in places a wild and untamed landscape that faces the full fury of ocean storms, but elsewhere, rugged headlands and fractured promontories protect coves, deep-water inlets and secluded landings where superb sandy beaches are backed by lush woodland.

Wild flowers, seabirds and seals are some of the constant draws, while the rocks span more than 700 million years of earth's history. Few places in Britain reveal such a concentration of geological drama. Inland there's plenty worth discovering too; the secretive reaches of the Daugleddau, where the gentle ebb and flow of the tide creates a rich feeding ground for waders, or wander onto the Preseli Hills, which have drawn man since before the Bronze Age.

Colourful Georgian houses surround Tenby's pretty harbour

Café and tea shop walks

Pembrokeshire's Café Culture is booming and it's not the big chains leading the way. Gone are the steamy fugs, greasy-spoon menus and chipped mugs; instead, there's no shortage of bright and friendly venues serving speciality coffees and teas, home-made baking, and wonderful snacks and meals that capitalise on the best of local produce and culinary talent. Very often there are take-away options too and sometimes interesting wines or Welsh-brewed beers and ciders. Many are open all day from breakfast and morning coffee to afternoon tea, with some venues running into the evening too with live music, poetry or storytelling. They are great places to rest or meet up with friends. So treat yourself and see what you can find — you'll not be disappointed.

"Tea amuses the evening, solaces the midnight and welcomes the morning."

Dr Samuel Johnson, 1760

TOP 10 **Walks:** Tea Shop walks

FOR MANY, WALKING AND REFRESHMENT GO NATURALLY HAND IN HAND and in Pembrokeshire you will find no shortage of delectable eating houses and enjoyable, scenic rambles that can be brought together to create this satisfying fusion. Combining the best of the countryside with fine food and local delicacies, inspired preparation and the warmth of Welsh hospitality, these ten superb rambles are crafted to create and feed a healthy outdoor appetite.

The Glasshouse Café
Cilgerran
page 8

Plumvanilla Café
Narberth
page

The Sound Café
St David's
page 20

The Boathouse Café
Dale
page

Garden Tearoom
St Ishmael's
page 32

Wavecrest Café
Angle
page 38

Quayside Tearoom
Lawrenny
page 42

Beach Break tearooms
Manorbier
page 46

Carne Vista
Tenby
page 52

Bothy Tearoom
Colby Garden
page 58

The Glasshouse Cafe occupies the top floor of the Welsh Wildlife Centre at Cilgerran

The Glasshouse Café

A wildlife reserve, river gorge and impressive medieval castle brought together in a delightful walk

What to expect:
Narrow, rugged and steep stepped paths within the gorge where care is required

Distance/time: 7 kilometres/ 4¼ miles. Allow 1½ to 2 hours

Start: Teifi Marsh Nature Reserve car park (pay and display)

Grid ref: SN 186 449

Ordnance Survey Map: OS Explorer OL35 (North Pembrokeshire)

Café: The Glasshouse Café, Welsh Wildlife Visitor Centre, Cilgerran A43 2TB | 01239 621600 | www.welshwildlife.org

Walk outline: The route through the gorge, past old quarry workings towards Cilgerran, is intriguing and pretty, but those less used to country walking may find its steeper stepped sections a challenge, particularly in poor weather. The return, however, is along good tracks and woodland paths and is far less demanding. Back at the visitor centre, you'll find wildlife displays, a gift shop and the Glasshouse Café.

Open all the year (apart from Christmas week), the Glasshouse Café's panoramic windows and open terrace give fantastic views across the reserve. The food is home-made from Fair Trade sourced and local produce.

Trails sign

☞ The Glasshouse Café at a glance

Open: Daily 10am - 5pm (10am - 4pm in winter). Closed Christmas week. Hot food served until 2:30pm

Food and specialities: The daily specials board highlights locally caught seafood, hearty meat dishes and imaginative fritters, pies and burgers. There's always home-made soup and light bites, from paninis to ploughmans, plus tempting cakes and tarts

Beverages: Speciality coffees, teas, infusions and hot chocolate as well as local bottled beers and ciders. Selection of wines and soft drinks

Children: Kids' healthy eating menu or smaller portions of main dishes

The Walk

1. Leave the **car park** by the ticket machine, branching left on the scenic path past the **visitor centre** to emerge near a giant **wicker badger**. *Adopted as an iconic symbol by the Wildlife Trust, the larger than life badger was created in 2013 by local willow weaver Michelle Cain, to symbolise the organisation's protection of the wider environment*

Turn right along the edge of a sloping meadow. Reaching another junction, double back right to a viewpoint overlooking the **river**.

The Welsh Wildlife Visitor Centre sits at the heart of the wonderful Teifi Marshes Nature Reserve, a 265 acre site which is home to a wide range of different habitats and an abundance of flora and fauna such as otters, kingfishers, badgers, deer and numerous wetland birds.

2. Retrace your steps, taking the second left, signed 'Gorge Trail'.

In addition to the walk through the gorge there are three other waymarked trails which reveal the many different aspects of the reserve including the reed beds, woodlands and open meadows.

Cross an intersecting wider track and continue with the path as it closes with the river.

Walk quietly beside the river and you might see an otter. Once common their numbers were

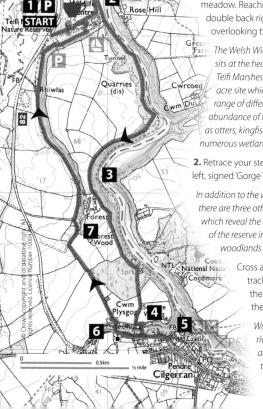

etland wonder: *A grey heron hunting for h at the reed margins*

pleted by hunting and loss of habitat, d they had become almost extinct in itain towards the end of the last century. t protection and improving water ality has seen populations once again crease along some of the country's rivers, here they live in holts amongst tree ots along the bank. Often solitary and rritorial, otters generally hunt at night, ding on fish, amphibians, crustaceans d occasional small mammals or birds.

Reaching another viewpoint by a **canoe store**, bear right. Stepped in its steepest sections, the path climbs and falls along the side of the **gorge**. At another fork, the easiest route lies with the permissive path to the right, the two paths re-uniting farther on. Again keep right, as the path later splits again, eventually rising to the lip of the gorge. Leaving the **nature reserve** through a gate, continue left on a broader track to its end by **Fforest Farm**.

3. Through the **small gate** on the left, a path carries on through trees, gently

Otter water?: *Sunlight and shadow on a tranquil stretch of the Afon Teifi*

losing height and eventually entering a **conifer plantation**. Rising from a **stream**, watch for the path bearing right to run at the plantation's perimeter. Ultimately leaving through a **kissing gate**, walk forward at the left edge of a large meadow.

4. Leave at the far end through a **kissing gate** onto a lane. Go left past a house, turning right immediately after on a descending path. Past a cottage, swing down to cross a **stream**, rising beyond to come out on **Church Street**. **Cilgerran** lies to the left, the **castle** reached along a short track off left towards its end.

5. Walk back along **Church Street**, passing **St Llawddog's Church**. Some 150 metres farther on, branch right down a short track. Over a **bridge**, clim between cottages to a metalled track at the top.

6. Cross diagonally left and follow a tra away. Bear right as another joins, walkir on to a small **parking area**. Keep ahead, passing through a **small gate** t continue briefly beside the main track.

7. The path then swings left, dropping to a junction in front of a field gateway.

ɾn right, passing through a gate to
ɪlow the lower edge of **woodland**.
ɪter 800 metres, keep right at a fork,
ɪying with the main path for another
ɪ0 metres. Coming to a junction

beside a **seat**, go left, crossing a service
drive to reach the **visitor centre** and
Glasshouse Café. Retrace your outward
steps to the car park to complete the
walk. ♦

Water Buffalo

Although natives of Asia, water buffalo have been grazing the boggy marshes of the Teifi Nature Reserve from early spring through to the start of winter since 2002. They thrive in the swampy environment and help prevent the spread of invasive bramble, gorse, willow and reedmace across the wet meadows, keeping the creeks and pools open for other wildlife such as birds, amphibians and the massive populations of damsel and dragonflies that are found here.

Plumvanilla Café promises imaginative food in a friendly, informal atmosphere

Plumvanilla Café

An easy walk through the pleasant, rolling countryside surrounding this pretty 'Landsker' town

What to expect:
Quiet lanes, tracks and footpaths, busy town streets

Distance/time: 3.25 kilometres/ 2 miles. Allow 1 to 1½ hours

Start: Town Moor car park, Narberth

Grid ref: SN 107 147

Ordnance Survey Map: OS Explorer OL36 (South Pembrokeshire)

Café: The Plumvanilla Café, St James Street, Narberth SA67 7DB | 01834 862762 | www.plumvanilla.com

Walk outline: From the Town Moor car park an old lane leads down through Plas Wood, later winding across the Mill Stream. Briefly emerging onto a narrow lane, the way climbs back through fields to the edge of town by St Andrew's Church. A short walk leads to the castle and then heads up Market Street to find Plumvanilla Café by the junction at the top. The final stretch follows the High Street back to the car park.

Rated one of the top ten budget restaurants and cafés in Pembrokeshire, Plumvanilla Café promises delicious, imaginative food in a bright and breezy, family-friendly atmosphere. The café is also renowned for its high quality, locally sourced food.

Chalkboard menu

The Plumvanilla Café at a glance

Open: Monday - Saturday 9-5pm

Food and Specialities: Asian and Moroccan cuisines are amongst those influencing the dishes created by Plum and served by Vanilla. Local, Fair Trade and organic foods are used wherever possible. Inventive vegetarian, as well as meat and fish dishes

Beverages: Speciality teas, coffees and fruit juices as well as wines and real beers

Children: Special menu for youngsters

The Walk

Narberth is well-known for its range of independent shops, cafes and restaurants and has also developed a reputation as an arts and antiques centre. In 2014 The Guardian called it 'not only a gastronomic hub for West Wales but also one of the liveliest, most likeable little towns in the UK'.

1. Leave **Town Moor car park** heading south-west and downhill through **Plas Wood** on a well-surfaced lane. This gradually descends through thick woodland, turning sharp left (ignore the signpost here, which points across open fields). The lane drops steeply to cross the small **Mill Stream** before heading up and onto a junction with a minor road.

Mill Stream is a tributary of the Eastern Cleddau ('Cleddau Ddu'), which joins with the Western Cleddau to form the Daugleddau and Milford Haven estuary. Milford Haven is deep, wide and sheltered — so much so that it forms an excellent natural harbour which can accommodate supertankers of 300,000 tonnes and more. Consequently, from 1957 it became an important centre of the oil industry, with Esso, BP, Texaco, Gulf Oil and Amoco all operating terminals and oil refineries here.

2. Turn left at this junction and follow the lane as it passes **Valley Farm** and **The Valley** on the right and descends to a kissing gate on the left. Go through this and across a field to a **concrete footbridge** over the same stream you crossed earlier in the walk.

0
0.5km
½ mile

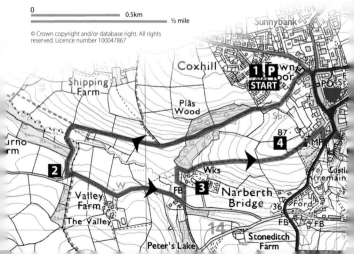

andsker fort: *Narberth Castle was partially emolished after the English Civil War*

Turn left on the far side of the bridge d follow the path with a fence on your jht and the stream on your left for bout 50 metres, then turn sharp right ross a field with a **water treatment ant** on your right to a kissing gate. te that the ground around the stream nk can be boggy in wet weather.

ss through the kissing gate into odland, going through a wooden te and crossing a small stream. ortly afterwards you emerge from

the woodland into a broad field with an indistinct grassy path heading diagonally uphill to the left. Follow this through the entrance to a second field (signposted) and head in the direction of **St Andrew's Church**.

St Andrew's Church dates back to the Middle Ages, although only the tower remains of the medieval church. The chancel was rebuilt in 1829 by James Hughes and the remainder of the church was rebuilt in 1881 by T.G. Jackson

4. You eventually come to a steel kissing gate; go through this and along a grassy

Relaxed town: *Galleries and gift shops abound on Narberth's pretty High Street*

bridleway towards **Plas Farm** on your left, where you'll see a gate and the church on your right. Pass through the gate and continue down the lane past **Narberth Bonded Stores** and the **town museum** on the left.

Narberth Museum is based in the Narberth Bonded Stores, a building originally designed to keep people out. Stored inside were hundreds of kegs full of duty-free whisky, brandy and rum. Only when the Revenue Officer and the Stores Manager were both present with their keys could the

double locks to the stores be opened — hence, today, the museum uses a symbol of two keys as its logo.

At the end of the lane turn left and wal up past **Market Square** and along **Hig Street** back to the car park to complete the walk.

Narberth is increasingly recognised for its annual food festival, held every Septembe It features a huge range of gourmet and local produce, along with live music, street theatre, cooking demonstrations, workshops and free children's activities.

For an optional (but worthwhile) detou to **Narberth Castle**, turn right at the

...nd of the lane for the short walk (150 ...etres) to explore the ruins.

...arberth Castle dates from Norman times ...d is mentioned in the Mabinogion. It ...as slighted by Oliver Cromwell following the English Civil War. The castle was opened to the public in 2005; at the opening ceremony, documents confirming the 'twinning' of Narberth and Ludlow were signed by the towns' mayors. ♦

The Landsker line

Narberth was founded around a Welsh court, but later became a Norman stronghold on the Landsker Line. Then and now the Landsker Line marked the language boundary between the mainly Welsh-speaking area to the north and the predominantly English-speaking area to the south, which is often known as 'Little England beyond Wales'. Many of the old Landsker churches feature distinctive defensive towers.

St Davids Cathedral was built in a hollow to hide it from Viking raiders

The Sound Café

A 'pilgrim' s' walk around the sacred places of St David's with a stunning section of coastal path

What to expect:
Field trods, rugged cliff paths, quiet lanes, and streets in St David's

Distance/time: 7 kilometres /4½ miles. Allow 2 to 2½ hours

Start: Porth Clais National Trust Car Park (Alternative start - St Davids Oriel y Parc car park (both pay and display)

Grid ref: SM 739 242

Ordnance Survey Map: OS Explorer OL35 (North Pembrokeshire)

Café: The Sound Café, 18 High Street, St David's SA62 6SD | 01437 721717

Walk outline: The walk leaves Porthclais, crossing coastal fields to St David's, where it winds through the old city past the Cathedral and Bishops' Palace. Continuing down the main street, the route turns beside Oriel y Parc and on along a lane toward the coast at Caerfai. Joining the Coast Path it winds round Pen y Cyfrwy to St Non's, continuing to St Non's bay and Porth y Ffynnon before turning into the inlet of Porth Clais.

Sitting on the High Street and one of St David's most vibrant haunts, The Sound Café is open all day for food and refreshment as well as hosting regular evening events when there's live music and open mike sessions too.

Service with a smile

The Sound Café at a glance

Open: Daily 9am - 5pm (10am - 4pm winter) and until 9pm on Wednesdays, Fridays and Saturdays when there's live music upstairs

Food and specialities: Everything from light snacks to full meals, with takeaway options too. Popular choices are the all-day breakfast, cawl and local crab sandwiches and there's a separate evening menu as well

Beverages: Extensive list of coffees, speciality teas, hot chocolate, milk shakes and soft drinks. Plus spirits, wines and Welsh bottled beers

Outside: You'll find tables in the front garden for when the sun shines

Children & dogs: Children's menus and smaller portions available, dogs allowed in garden seating area

The Walk

1. Leaving the **car park**, go left along the lane, crossing the **stream** behind **Porth Clais harbour**.

The natural harbour of Porth Clais has long served as a safe haven, and was one of the many spots linking the trading and early religious communities of Ireland and Britain. It was here that Bishop Elvis landed from Ireland, baptising St David in a spring that spontaneously burst from the hill, and many pilgrims subsequently made landfall at Porth Clais on their journey to visit the shrines at St David's Cathedral.

Leave on the bend just beyond, climbing a stepped path through thick scrub on the right. At the top, keep ahead across grazing and then at the edge of a **camping field** to **Porthclais Farm**. Entering the **yard**, swing left along a track, but almost immediately turn off through a gate on the right. A path leads away beside a couple of fields and then between banks for a good 800 metres. Keep ahead as another path joins from the right to emerge at a junction by **Warpool Court Hotel**.

2. The lane to the left leads into **St David's**, becoming a street as it bends past houses. Keep ahead to the end and there go left. After 200 metres, opposite another junction, turn right along a

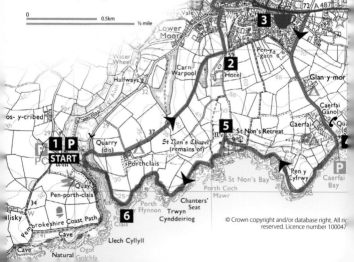

© Crown copyright and/or database right. All rights reserved. Licence number 100047

heltered water: *A sturdy breakwater rotects the natural harbour at Porthclais*

metalled track to the **Bishop's Palace nd Cathedral**.

t David's Cathedral dates from 1176, hen it was rebuilt following destruction y Viking raiders and was an important ilgrimage site throughout the Middle ges. Restored by the Victorian architect r George Gilbert Scott, it is again a magnificent building, containing the cently renovated shrine of St David. otable too are a magnificent rood screen,

15th-century misericords in the choir and an impressive beamed roof over the nave fashioned from Irish bog oak.

On the opposite bank of the River Alun are the ruins of the Bishop's Palace, constructed in the latter part of the 13th century by Bishop Bek. The Reformation brought decline and when Bishop Barlow left in 1536, he took with him the lead from the roof, reputedly to fund dowries for his five daughters. The bishopric moved its seat to Abergwilli and the building was eventually abandoned. It is now in the care of CADW.

Complex geology: *Sea caves, arches and islands on the far side of Caerfai Bay*

Having explored the ecclesiastical precincts, climb the **Thirty-nine Steps** from the south front of the Cathedral. Turn left through an arch and follow the street into **the square** at the centre of **St David's**. Walk forward along **High Street** to the **Sound Café** on the right.

3. Continue beyond, turning in past the **Oriel y Parc Gallery** to emerge beyond on **Fford Caerfai** opposite the entrance to a **car park**. Turn right and follow it for 1 kilometre to the **car park** at **Caerfai Bay**.

4. Keep ahead to find the **Coast Path** leaving at the far side. Follow it away above the cliffs to the right to **St Non's** about 1 kilometre away. Approaching St Non's, take the right fork, below the retreat and small **chapel**, (open to the public). **St Non's Well** can be found in the south west corner of the garden, while in the field beyond, the **ruin of the original chapel** can be seen.

5. A trod leads past the ruin to regain the **Coast Path** over a stile. Continue along the coast to the right.

6. Eventually the path turns in to the narrow inlet of **Porth Clais**, its mouth protected by a sturdy harbour wall. Jus╵

...eyond the point, a path drops to the **...arbour**, but the Coast Path remains ...gh above the inlet. Farther on, at ...ork, bear left descending above a ...ouple of **lime kilns** to the head of the ...tuary and out onto a lane.

The old kilns were built to burn limestone landed from Carew, which was then spread across the fields as a fertiliser.

Turn left and walk back to the car park to complete the walk. ◆

St Non's chapel

Lying within a ring of pagan stones, the ruins mark the traditional site of St David's birth to St Non in AD520. Standing beside a sacred healing spring, it later became a place of medieval pilgrimage. The nearby chapel to Our Lady and St Non was built as a private chapel for the house in 1934, which was subsequently taken over by the Passionist Fathers to be run as a religious retreat.

Descending grassy steps towards kxx

The Boathouse Café

The circuit of St Ann's Head, which guards the narrow entrance to Milford Haven, reveals arresting views

What to expect:
Good clifftop and field edge paths, quiet lanes at the start and finish, several ups and downs during the first half

Distance/time: 11 kilometres/ 7 miles. Allow 3 to 3½ hours

Start: Public car park (pay and display) at Dale

Grid ref: SM 810 058

Ordnance Survey Map: OS Explorer OL36 (South Pembrokeshire)

Café: The Boathouse Café, Dale SA62 3RB | 01437 721717

Walk outline: Beginning behind the beach at Dale, the route follows a wooded lane towards Dale Point. Crossing the neck of the narrow promontory, it rejoins the coast and continues past a succession of sandy bays to the lighthouses on St Ann's Head. After following the rugged western flank of the Dale peninsula the way turns back across the fields to the car park.

The Boathouse is a traditional family café. Looking straight out over Dale's superb beach, it provides everything from ice creams and steaming tea to full meals cooked to order. The integral convenience shop is an Aladdin's Cave of beach toys, gifts and basic foods as well as all those essentials you forgot to bring along.

Friendly staff

The Boathouse Café at a glance

Open: Daily 10am - 5pm. Easter until the end of September

Food and Specialities: All day breakfast, burgers, fish dishes, curries, chilli and a range of baps, paninis, sandwiches and more are all available with chips and salads, with puddings or Upton ice cream to follow if you have room. They'll also pack a lunch or afternoon snack to take away

Outside: There's ample seating on the forecourt beside the beach

Children & dogs: Children's menus cater for smaller appetites. Dogs permitted to forecourt tables; inside only at owner's discretion

Accommodation: Holiday let available

The Walk

1. Turn right from the **car park** and follow the shore road through **Dale**. Keeping left at successive junctions past the **Boathouse Café**, climb away along a leafy lane. After a kilometre, having left the woods behind and nearing the **Dale Fort Field Centre**, watch for the **Coast Path** leaving through a gate on the right.

2. Walk away beside the bank of a ditch, the defences of an **Iron Age promontory fort**. Farther east are the landward defences of a **Victorian fort** that overlooks the mouth of Milford Haven. The path winds on at the field edge before losing height through trees to cross a **stream** at the head of **Castlebeach Bay**. Climb past the overgrown ruin of a **lime kiln**, shortly breaking from the leafy cover and following the perimeter of fields to a tall **navigation tower** on **Watwick Point**.

sherman's friend: The pontoon jetty at ale rises and falls with the tide

Keep going above the coast. Towards e far corner of the third field, the path aves left to wind above the head of atwick Bay. At a fork, the left branch ops steeply to the beach, an idyllic ot more than amply justifying the mb back. The ongoing path continues West Blockhouse Point where, as name suggests, there is a **Victorian** ockhouse as well as three more vigation markers.

4. Skirt them on the landward side and then pass **gun emplacements** on your right. The onward way follows the sweep of **Mill Bay**, crossing a couple of streams at its head. Regain height and walk on at the field edge, watching for a **stone marker** commemorating Henry Tudor's landing from France in 1485. Approaching the settlement on **St Ann's Head**, leave the field through a gate and follow a path past **walled gardens** that once fed the small community, continuing beyond the corner toward the **lighthouse**. Reaching a fence, swing

Ancient site: *Dale Castle is a remodelled medieval fortress overlooking Dale Roads*

---

right past the **lighthouse cottages** and on beside a drive to arrive at the compound gate.

Henry Tudor is said to have founded a chapel on St Ann's Head to acknowledge his safe landfall from France in Mill Bay, just two weeks before defeating Richard III at Bosworth Field in 1485. It provided the first light to guide mariners into The Haven before a purpose-built beacon was erected around 1650. Today's twin lighthouses were built in 1714; the northern light is now redundant, but the other, re-sited in *1841 because of erosion, continues as the base station controlling the automatic operation of all Pembroke's lighthouses.*

5. First take the path opposite, which leads to a **viewpoint** above a tiny cove where the rock has been dramatically folded. Return to the track and follow it left past the **old lighthouse**. Emerging through the outer gateway, branch off left with the **Coast Path** to follow the cliffs above **Frenchman's Bay** and **Welshman's Bay**. Beyond **Great Castle Head**, the site of an Iron Age promontory fort, the path drops to the head of **Westdale Bay**.

Turn inland along the base of a shallow valley towards **Dale village**. Through a gate, join a track that runs forward to meet the corner of a lane. Again keep ahead, shortly passing the church. After a farther 200 metres, watch for a gate on the right. Head away across the field. Entering the next field, bear left to reach the lane behind **The Boathouse Café**. Continue left to reach the car park and complete the walk. ♦

Dale Fort

During the middle of the 19th century, Napoleon was a credible threat to Britain, and numerous forts and gun batteries were raised at strategic locations around the coast. The fort at Dale was one of fifteen built within The Haven to protect the naval dockyards at Pembroke, and occupies the site of an Iron Age encampment. Paired with Thorn Island across the sound, it would have presented a formidable defence to any attempted attack.

Stepping stones cross the tidal pill at Sandy Haven

Garden Tearoom

Fine sands at low tide and a succession of tiny bays are delights along one of The Haven's less-visited sections

What to expect:
Quiet lanes, tracks and coast path

Distance/time: 10 kilometres/ 6 miles. Allow 2½ to 3 hours

Start: St Ishmael's Garden Centre car park

Grid ref: SM 828 074

Ordnance Survey Map: OS Explorer OL36 (South Pembrokeshire)

Café: Garden Tearoom, St Ishmael's SA62 3SX | 01646 636343 | www.stishmaelsgardencentre.com

Walk outline: The inland section follows quiet lanes, leading to the pretty, wooded inlet of Sandyhaven Pill, where low tide reveals a fine beach. Joining the Coast Path, the return winds around successive headlands, all used as defensive positions at one time or another. Turning in along the pretty valley behind Monk Haven, the way passes an ancient church before picking up the lane back to St Ishmael's Garden Centre.

A shaded patio garden and cosy indoor area with sofas by the fire give this bright café a lovely atmosphere. Relax after the walk and wander round the garden centre, which as well as plants and garden accessories stocks leisure clothing, crafts and pictures.

Tempting menu board

The Garden Tearoom at a glance

Open: Daily from 9am - 5pm (4pm in winter) – note car park closes with the café

Food and Specialities: Menu includes all day breakfasts, home made soups and crusty bread, ham and home made burgers, filled local jacket potatoes, salads, Welsh rarebit and a mouthwatering selection of cakes

Outside: Covered patio garden area

Children & dogs: There's a children's menu and dogs are allowed in the patio area

The Walk

1. Head south from the **garden centre**, keeping left at a junction to **St Ishmael's**. Stay with the main lane through the **village**, passing **The Brook Inn** and **school**. After some 800 metres, at a junction, go through the field gate ahead and walk on with the high hedge bank on your left. Slip through a gate partway along to continue with it on your right, shortly reaching **Sandy Haven Farm**. Leave the fields over a stile and carry on beside a high stone wall to the **farmyard**. Wind right and left out onto a lane. Go right and then at the next junction turn left down to **Sandy Haven**.

Although the Coast Path across the sand at Sandy Haven is innocuous enough at low tide, high water completely floods the ria and walkers must wait for the ebb or face a lengthy inland trek. It is a delightful spot and was one of the places in the area that inspired the artist Graham Sutherland, some of whose works are displayed at the Oriel y Parc at St David's.

2. Retrace your steps up the hill, watching for the **Coast Path** leaving on the left up steps and through a gate. Wind through trees and continue beyond at the edge of fields. Carry on

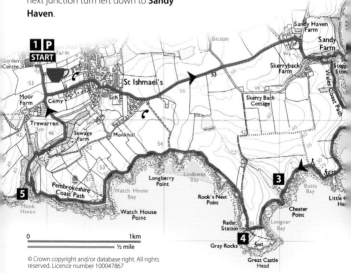

...ummer shores: *A walker enjoys the view ...long the coast to Great Castle Head*

...bove the low cliffs, rounding **Little ...astle Head** to pass a tall **navigation ...arker** above **Butts Bay**.

... The path winds on behind **Longoar ...ay** towards **Great Castle Head**. There, ... cuts inland across the neck of the ...romontory beside the bank of an **Iron ...ge fortification** to meet a track. The ...uildings over to the left house a **radar ...ation**, which helps control navigation ... shipping in the Milford Haven roads.

The tall beacon just west of Little Castle Head is one of several lights erected to help guide shipping into The Haven. Submerged offshore shoals make the approach difficult and tugs escort the LNG (Liquefied Natural Gas) and oil tankers to the jetties lining the deepwater inlet. Nevertheless the last 50 years have seen two major disasters in the groundings of the Donna Marika in 1973 and the Sea Empress in 1996, the latter spilling some 73,000 tonnes of crude oil which resulted in a massive loss of sea birds and polluted 125 miles of coastline.

Leafy crossing: *Sandy Haven is one of Pembrokeshire's more atmospheric inlets*

4. Briefly follow the track right, again watching for the **Coast Path** signed off to the left. The route undulates gently above a curving succession of coves separated by stubby promontories. At the far end is **Watch House Point**, where hidden amongst the bramble and gorse above the path are the remains of **open-fronted shelters** that housed a Second World War artillery battery. Beyond the path gently falls towards Monk's Haven. Passed on the way is an impressive watch tower, which although appearing medieval, is in fact a **Victorian folly**. Wind down to the tiny cove of **Monk's Haven**.

5. Swing right over a **bridge** behind a **high stone wall** at the back of the beach to a three-way signpost. Leave the coast path, following the inland path up the valley. Higher up, go right in front of a gate to wind around the walls of **Monk Haven Manor**. Emerging onto the corner of a surfaced track by the **church**, keep ahead and continue straight up the lane beyond.

St Ishmael came from Cornwall, a disciple of St David and his successor as Bishop of St David's. The church, which bears his name, dates from 1100. Instead of a towe

a double bellcote is to be seen above its western wall and look too for three incised medieval stones. The massive wall across the head of the beach however is 'modern', built around 1840 as part of the Trewarren House estate.

Walk on past successive junctions, eventually returning to the **garden centre** and **tearoom** to complete the walk. ♦

Wartime Defences

Facing the entrance to Milford Haven, Watch House Point was a strategic location during the Second World War on which searchlight, artillery and anti aircraft batteries were sited. Further defences were laid on the shore below in the form of a minefield and barbed wire fences. The area around Sandy Haven was used as a 'Starfish' decoy, where fires, flares and lights were set to lure enemy bombers away from the docks of The Haven.

The vast, open beach at Freshwater West is popular with surfers

Wavecrest Café

Wonderful walking along a rugged coast, overlooking wave battered cliffs and a succession of rocky coves

What to expect:
Rough clifftop paths with many ups and downs, the return stretch is along quiet lanes

Distance/time: 14 kilometres/ 8½ miles. Allow 4 to 4½ hours

Start: Public car park overlooking southern end of Freshwater West

Grid ref: SR 885 998

Ordnance Survey Map: OS Explorer OL36 (South Pembrokeshire)

Café: Wavecrest Café, Angle SA71 5BE | 01646 641457 | www.wavecrestangle.co.uk

Walk outline: The walk begins along the broad strand of Freshwater West before climbing onto the cliffs of the southern flank of the Angle peninsula. Rounding Rat Island, the way drops to the Wavecrest Café. After cutting inland along a lane to Angle village, there's a stretch beside Angle Bay, following a private drive above the shore. The route then turns up over the neck of the Angle peninsula, dropping back to the coast.

Angle beach might have been without a café for three years, but the arrival of Wavecrest in 2014 has put this superb little bay back on the map. This delightful café is well worth visiting in its own right for imaginative food and friendly service.

Wavecrest wonders

🍴 The Wavecrest Café at a glance

Open: Daily 11am - 5pm (11am- 4pm in winter)

Food and Specialities: Well-presented good food, all home-made with a range of appetising dishes, many featuring local fish, crab and lobster. Pop by on a winter Sunday and you can enjoy a traditional roast dinner

Beverages: As well as freshly ground coffee and speciality teas, there's a range of wines, local beers or even in summer a pitcher of Pimms

Dogs: Dogs allowed at outside tables and in winter, a small indoor eating area is available. Doggie snacks and water is available

Children: Children's menus and smaller portions of many dishes

The Walk

1. Cross to the **beach** and head north (with the sea on your left) below the dunes. Nearing rocks at the far end, look for a path turning inland, which soon swings left to meander along low cliffs above a succession of rugged coves. Near the **natural arch of Guttle Hole** is a crumbling **tower**, perhaps an early lighthouse or watchtower. The path winds on, skirting **Whitedole Bay** to a promontory overlooking **Sheep Island**.

3. Rounding the fort, the path winds on, shortly following the edge of successive fields before finally dropping to the head of the beach by the **Wavecrest Café**.

4. Follow the lane inland through **Angle village**.

5. Where the road swings to the right at the far end of the village, keep ahead on a narrow leafy lane. Carry on through a gate as it becomes a private drive, which skirts the back of Angle Bay. Eventually the drive swings off to the right, but keep ahead just little farther with the **Coast Path** to find a track off to

2. Beyond the promontory, carry on above **Castles Bay**, shortly turning in above **Welcome Pit**, an impressive blowhole breaking the sandstone cliff.

nhurried inlet: *Boats moored close to ngle village, in Angle Bay*

ne right. Walk on as it becomes a lane, ortly meeting a junction.

Go left for 400 metres to find a path aving over a stile by a field gate on the ght. If you reach the white-towered **ocket Cart Cottage**, you've gone too far. Walk along the field edge. Passing into a second field, bear left to a stile at the far side. Drop to a **stream** in a small valley and turn right towards the coast. Crossing a stile at the bottom, rejoin the **Coast Path** and follow it left, reversing your outward route across **Freshwater West** beach back to the car park, to complete the walk. ♦

Surfers' paradise?

With a half-mile run of dune-backed beach, Freshwater West is an inviting spot, but a strong rip current can pull the unwary out to sea — making swimming dangerous. However, those same conditions make it one of the finest surfing beaches in the country. On the best days, the surf yields world class sport and it has become a popular venue for the Welsh National Surfing Championships, occurring over the first May bank holiday.

Quayside Tearooms' tables overlook a lovely reach of the Daugleddau

Quayside Tearooms

idden amongst the quiet, upper reaches of the
augleddau, Lawrenny Quay was once a bustling port

What to expect:
Woodland and field
paths, quiet lanes

istance/time: 5 kilometres/ 3 miles. Allow 1½ to 2 hours

art: Parking by Quayside Tearoom, Lawrenny Quay

rid ref: SN 010 062

rdnance Survey Map: OS Explorer OL36 (South Pembrokeshire)

aroom: Quayside, Lawrenny Quay SA68 0PR| 01646 641457 |
ww.quaysidelawrenny.co.uk

alk outline: From Lawrenny Quay, the walk heads across
loping, oak-clad hillside overlooking a narrowing reach of
e Daugleddau. After turning in above Garron Pill, the route
scends to the shore, leaving the estuary along a narrow lane
o Lawrenny village. Turning beside the church, the path
mbs a low hill to more outstanding views over the water
fore dropping through woodland back to the café.

e Quayside is run by the same husband and wife team as the
avecrest at West Angle; expect equally sumptuous food, attention
detail and a warm welcome. The lawn tables look out over the
er – an ideal spot to relax as boats come and go on the tide.

Quayside Tearooms

The Quayside Tearoom at a glance

en: Daily 11am - 5pm between Easter and September

od and Specialities: Specialising in well-presented good food, all
me-made with a range of appetising dishes, many featuring local fish,
o and lobster. Salads come with Quayside's own special dressing

verages: As well as freshly ground coffee, speciality teas and infusions
re's a range of wines, local beers or Pimms in summer

gs: Dogs permitted in lawn areas; doggie snacks and water available.

ldren: Children's menus and smaller portions available

The Walk

1. Follow the metalled track past the **Quayside Tearooms** into a **boatyard**. Going left, pass through and keep ahead over a crossing track into the trees. Bend right in front of the entrance to a cottage, rising to a gate. The ongoing path undulates across the slope of a delightful wooded heath above **Castle Reach**. Keep going for 1.2 kilometres until the path emerges into a small clearing above the mouth of **Garron Pill**, where a disused hut once served as a hide.

2. Wind through to continue a little farther within the trees above the inlet before reaching a redundant stile. There, turn down **steps** to the **stony shore** and pick your way along it to the right. If the tide is in, you may have to wait a short while for the ebb. Before long, a track develops, which leads out to a lane.

3. Follow the lane right over a low hill, falling beyond the crest into **Lawrenny**. As the lane bends towards a junction, turn off right through a gate immediately beside the entrance to **Lawrenny church**.

4. Head away below the **graveyard**, passing through a gap in a **broken wall** to walk at the top edge of a second

small pasture. Through another gap, curve right to climb beside a fence on the left, from which there are splendid views across the confluence of the Carew and Cresswell rivers.

5. Through a **kissing gate** at the top corner, continue at the edge of a couple more fields beside the estate wall. Leaving through another **kissing gate** at the far end, carry on along a

*et and dry: Heading along the muddy
argins of Garron Pill at low tide*

...scending path through woodland to
...e river.

...uring the 18th century, Lawrenny
...ospered from fishing, boat-building
...d the transhipment of limestone
...d coal brought down by barge from
...ndshipping and Cresswell onto

sea-going vessels, while its oysters were
sent to Bristol and London where they
were considered 'the fattest, whitest and
sweetest'.

6. Emerging opposite the **Lawrenny
Arms**, follow the metalled drive right,
back to the parking area and the
Quayside Tearooms to complete the
walk. ♦

St Caradoc's Church, Lawrenny

*Born to a wealthy family and influential at court, St
Caradoc forsook worldly power for the humble life of a
monk. He lived as a hermit on Barry Island and later at
Haroldston, finally being buried at St David's Cathedral
in 1124. St Caradoc's Church, founded shortly after and
dedicated to him, owes its present appearance to the
Victorian largesse of the Lort-Phillips family who lived in
the now-demolished Lawrenny Castle.*

Manorbier Castle seen from the Wales Coast Path

Beach Break tearooms

'In all the broad land of Wales, Manorbier is the most pleasant place by far' — said 'Gerald of Wales' in 1146

What to expect:
Cliff and field paths, narrow lanes and tracks

Distance/time: 4 kilometres/ 2½ miles. Allow 1½ to 2 hours

Start: Public car park (pay and display) behind beach at Manorbier

Grid ref: SS 063 976

Ordnance Survey Map: OS Explorer OL36 (South Pembrokeshire)

Teashop: Beach Break tearooms, Manorbier SA70 7TD | 01834 871709 | www.beachbreaktearooms.co.uk

Walk outline: After heading down to the beach, the route takes to the low, but quite spectacular cliffs around Priest's Nose, passing the impressive remains of an ancient burial chamber. Above Presipe Bay, the way climbs inland past Hill Farm, joining a track in the valley beyond, which leads to Manorbier village, where you will find The Beach Break tearooms. The return is via the hilltop church of St James, though you may alternatively visit Manorbier Castle.

You'll easily spot the brightly painted Beach Break, which is as much a local craft shop as it is tearoom; for all the quality ornaments and pictures on the shelves and walls are for sale.

Beach Break tearooms

The Beach Break tearooms at a glance

Open: February through to November, 9am-6pm during the season, otherwise 10am-5pm

Food and Specialities: All food is prepared on the premises using produce from nearby farms and local producers. Firm favourites are cawl, smoked salmon and prawn salads, and locally cured bacon

Beverages: A wide range of teas, infusions and own-blend coffee plus cakes, smoothies and other drinks. Welsh beers and wine

Children: Children's menu, including a healthy eating snack box.

Dogs: Welcome at pavement tables or in secluded rear garden

The Walk

1. Paths leave the **car park** heading down to the bay. There, bear left behind beach to pick up the **Coast Path**, which rises onto low cliffs. *Not far along is a small but impressive cromlech, an ancient burial chamber known as **King's Quoit**.*

2. Carry on beyond towards the point of **Priests Nose**, passing a couple of dramatically **narrow chasms**, *which have been eroded by the sea from softer layers embedded within the vertical layers of Old Red Sandstone strata.*

Rounding the point, the view in front is to the bold prominence of **Old Castle Head**, *the site of a prehistoric fort, but now occupied by the Royal Artillery.* The ongoing path runs above a steepening, grassy slope that falls to low cliffs, broken by a succession of tiny, rock-strewn coves. After gaining height onto a small **headland**, the path turns in behind **Presipe Bay**, the path leading to a gate at the back.

3. Leave the coast at that point and climb away at the field edge. Cresting the rise, swing right towards **Hill Farm** and skirt the farm on a field track. As it then bends at the side, leave over a stile on the right. Head downhill across successive fields, leaving at the bottom through a gap.

4. The way back lies to the left over a stile. Follow the ongoing track past a **cottage**. Joining with a track from Hill Farm, it continues right into the **village of Manorbier**. Reaching a junction at the end, the **Beach Break Tearooms** lie just to the right.

5. Leaving the tearooms, walk back pas[t] the track by which you

Coastal sentinel: *Looking out to sea from one of Manobier Castle's round towers*

...tered the village to a fork just beyond. ...you want to visit the **castle**, bear right ... find the entrance beside the **war memorial**.

...unded by the Norman knight, Odo de ...rri, who was awarded the manor for his ...vices during the Conquest, Manorbier's ...stle is remarkably complete and brings ...gether the stark fortifications that were ...cessary to secure the submission of the ...al Welsh with a degree of medieval

comfort and convenience for the lord. Although originally a simple earth motte, what we see today is largely the work of his son William, its curtain walls enclosing a substantial inner ward and having two gates, one of which led down to the sea. The de Barris played a prominent role in the subsequent Norman expansion across the Irish Sea, being rewarded again with extensive grants of land in Ireland. The castle here remained with the family until the 15th century, being attacked only once during that time, ironically by a de Barri in a family fall-out over succession.

Historic landfall: *Manorbier Castle and St James' church guard the bay*

Three hundred years later it fell to the Parliamentarians during the English Civil Wars and was subsequently slighted and abandoned.

Most remembered of the family today is Odo's fourth grandson, Giraldus Cambrensis, also known as Gerald of Wales. Born in 1145, unlike his brothers who followed careers in the military, he was encouraged to enter the Church. He studied in the Benedictine abbey of St Peter's in Gloucester and was then sent to St David's, where his uncle was Bishop. Gerald distinguished himself by exposing corruption in the Welsh Church and was rewarded by appointment as archdeacon of Brecon. However, his sight. were firmly set on succeeding his uncle to the bishopric of St David's, and although offered other positions of rank, much of h subsequent life was spent in unsuccessful efforts to promote his cause. After repeate rejection, he retired to academic study and writing, penning amongst other things accounts of his travels in Wales an Ireland. Giraldus was of Norman-Welsh descent, his mother being Nest ferch Rhys the only legitimate daughter of Rhys ap Gruffydd, the last king of South Wales ana his works offer an insight to medieval life and the relationship of the Welsh to their

orman overlords. His 'Tour of Wales' is full
f humour and incisive observation, and
emains a good read today.

therwise, keep left down the hill back
owards the coast. However, a short

distance along, a lane off on the left
climbs to **St James' Church**, from which
there is a fine view across the foot of the
valley. A path then drops back to the **car
park** to complete the walk. ♦

King's Quoit

*Perched on two remaining uprights, the mighty
capstone of the King's Quoit cantilevers towards the back
of the bay. Legend says that it was hurled by a powerful
king, but who he was and the circumstances have long
been forgotten. The facts are equally elusive; Neolithic
dolmens appear across the Old World and although
assumed to be burial sites, may have served other
functions too such as meeting places or tribal markers.*

Pastel-hued houses in Tenby's 'Old Town' reflected in the tranquil harbour

Caffè Vista

Two of Wales' most picturesque beach resorts in Wales are linked by this fantastic coastal walk

What to expect:
A linear walk from Saundersfoot to Tenby. Undulating coastal path

Distance/time: 6.5 kilometres/ 4 miles. Allow 2 to 2½ hours

Start: Long stay car park in Upper Park Road, Tenby and catch No. 352 or 381 bus outside to begin the walk from Saundersfoot

Grid ref: SN 133 003

Ordnance Survey Map: OS Explorer OL36 (South Pembrokeshire)

Café: Caffè Vista, Tenby SA70 7HA | 01834 849636

Walk outline: Leave the car in Tenby, and catch the bus to Saundersfoot. Join the Coast Path there, from where it undulates along wooded cliffs to Monkstone Point and its sheltered beach. The way dips across Lodge Valley, then winds behind Waterwynch before finally reaching Tenby, where there's plenty to explore around the harbour, Castle Hill and old town.

Caffè Vista is tucked off the High Street in Crackwell Street, its unpretentious frontage belying the splendid view over the harbour and North Beach from its balcony terrace. Tenby's first (and reputedly best) espresso bar has a distinct Greek influence and serves an appetising selection of snacks and light meals.

Superb coffee and tea

🍃 Caffè Vista at a glance

Open: Daily 9-5pm

Food and Specialities: The passion for coffee extends to the food, with Greek specialities and delicious pastries, cakes and ice creams all crafted from local produce. In summer a more extensive menu including steak and fish dishes is available from the Sailing Club by the harbour

Outside: Small terrace overlooking North Beach

Children & dogs: Children welcome and dogs permitted in small lounge area or on terrace

Evenings: Evening acoustic concerts featuring jazz, blues and folk musicians from around the world

The Walk

1. Buses leave **Tenby** by the **car park** in **Upper Park Road**.

2. Alighting from the bus in **Saundersfoot**, make your way onto the **harbour car park**. Turn right past the **sluice** and then swing left along the **southern quay**. At the corner, drop to continue along the **beach**. After 250 metres look for **steps** that emerge on **The Glen** beside **Rhode Wood**. At high tide, instead follow the main road (**B4316**) towards Tenby, swinging left and right up **St Brides Hill**. At the top, take the second of two streets on the left, **The Glen**, and head down to a bend where the beach path joins.

3. The **Coast Path** winds up into **Rhode Wood**, continuing along the cliffs for almost 800 metres before dropping into a fold. A path off left gives access to the beach, but the route continues ahead, over a **plank bridge** and back onto the cliffs.

4. After later briefly breaking to the field edge there is a junction, where a path off left leads out across the flank of **Monkston Point** to return along its crest. Just beyond, a sign indicates a steep access to the beach below. However, the **Coast Path** remains high at the field edge, shortly winding behind a **wireless mast**. Further

0   1km
           1 mile

Holiday heaven?: *Pleasure craft crowd Saundersfoot's busy old harbour*

n, re-entering trees, the way drops once more to the foot of **Lodge Valley**. Keep with the path ahead to regain the cliff tops before swinging inland above **Waterwynch**. Losing height, cross a couple of **streams** to arrive at a junction above **Waterwynch House**.

. Cross the drive to the continuing path opposite, which leads to the beach. However, the **Coast Path** leaves first ght up **Waterwynch Lane**, the path

climbing over a final hill to **Tenby**. Keep going as it becomes a lane, entering the town along a **marine drive** above Tenby's **North Beach**. At the end, go left along **High Street** and keep left into **Crackwell Street**, where you will find **Caffé Vista**. Keep going beyond to the **harbour** to **Castle Hill**, where a path leads around the promontory passing Tenby's present and former **lifeboat stations**.

From almost any vantage looking out across North Beach to St Catherine's Island, Tenby presents a perfect picture with rows of

Summer delight: *Tenby Old Town and its pretty harbour in high summer*

brightly painted Georgian houses vying for the best view. Its Welsh name, Dinbych-y-Pysgod translates as the 'little fort of the fishes' and reflects Tenby's early history as a busy Viking fishing village. Even then, a fortress was deemed necessary to defend its trade, but the arrival of the Normans saw the construction of a stout castle on the high promontory that cups the northern sands and looks back over the town. Little remains of it today, but sections of the town walls, successively added to over the following centuries

remain impressive, in particular The Five Arches barbican. That it survives is due to the foresight of the late 18th-century Doctor Charter, who fought against its demolition by Thomas Paxton. Paxton had conceived a bold plan to develop Tenby as a spa and, walls apart, his endeavours paid off, for the town remains an attractive and popular resort today, counting Roald Dahl amongst its more distinguished visitors who enjoyed boyhood holidays here. Places not to miss include the National Trust's Tudor Merchant's House. Dating from the 15th century, it is Tenby's oldest residence and is furnished to depict the life of a prosperous merchant family

. Return along **Crackwell Street**, turning off left up **Quay Hill** past the Tudor Merchant's House (NT). Go right along **St Julian's Street** and then left before **St Mary's Church**. The first right, **St George's Street** leads through to the **Five Arches Gate**. Turn right to find **Upper Park Road** and the **car park** then off on the left (Waypoint **1**) to complete the walk. ♦

St Mary's Church, Tenby

The soaring tower and spire of St Mary's Church would have provided a distinctive landmark to mariners in the days when Tenby was a busy port. Perhaps originally a Norman foundation, it was much added to in the 15th century. Its most impressive feature is the wagon roof and panelled ceiling, adorned with 75 carved bosses. Look out for Jesus and the four Evangelists, strange grotesques and a Green Man.

Enjoying tea and cake outside at the National Trust's Colby Woodland Gardens

Bothy Tearoom

What to expect:
Undulating coastal and woodland paths and tracks

Two delightful wooded valleys and a superb walled garden and summerhouse feature in this enjoyable walk

Distance/time: 6.5 kilometres/ 4 miles. Allow 1½ to 2 hours

Start: Amroth Car Park, off Brookside Villas, by Amroth Arms SA67 8NQ

Grid ref: SN 162 070

Ordnance Survey Map: OS Explorer OL35 (North Pembrokeshire)

Café: Bothy Tearoom at Colby Woodland Garden SA67 8PP | 01834 811885

Walk outline: After following coastal cliffs to the beach at Wiseman's Bridge, the route winds inland along Pleasant Valley. Rising over higher ground, the way continues beside fields and through woodland to Colby where the gardens and tearoom offer a fine excuse to break the journey. The final stretch is an easy walk along the wooded Summerhill valley back to the coast.

Bringing the former estate work sheds and stables back to life, the Bothy Tearoom is a great place to pause for a snack or full meal, where all the food is home-made and freshly cooked to order. You can browse the craft gallery and second-hand bookstall and visit the beautiful walled garden and wonderful summerhouse.

Box hedge-lined 'rill'

The Bothy Tearoom at a glance

Open: Daily 10-4:30pm Easter until the end of October half-term

Food and Specialities: Cured meats, Welsh cheeses, slow roasted pork and special flans are served with tasty salads and home-made chutneys. Speciality teas and coffee accompanies delicious cakes, and if you fancy something stronger, there's a selection of local beers, cider and wine.

Outside: There're tables in the courtyard for when the sun shines.

Dogs: Dogs are allowed at the courtyard tables, or when wet, in the information room

The Walk

1. Head out to the **sea front** and go right. Leave the road at the end of the **promenade**, climbing away through trees behind a **toilet block**. Emerging at the top, carry on through a meadow. Watch for a sign part way along directing you right to a gate.

2. Coming out onto a **metalled track**, follow it left. As it eventually develops as a lane, keep going downhill to reach the **coast** beside the **Wiseman's Bridge Inn**. Walk on behind the **beach**, crossing a **bridge** over a stream at the far end.

As with many places along the Pembrokeshire coast, a warming climate 10,000 years ago released immense quantities of meltwater, which gouged deep valleys across the landscape as it escaped to the sea. Those behind both Amroth and Wiseman's Bridge exposed layers of coal, which have been exploited since at least the beginning of the 17th century.

The seams were initially worked from simple bell pits and then later, from deepe

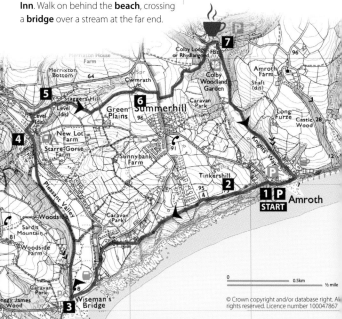

eltered shore: *The broad, sandy beach at* 'semans Bridge*

afts and levels, which followed the coal
ep into the hillside. Although the seams
ere thin, the coal was of such quality that
vas much valued and during the 19th
ntury was shipped around the world to
nker the Royal Navy's fleet. At first the
al was exported on small ships, beached
loading at low tide.

demand increased, a mineral railway
s built from the mines and along the
st to the harbour at Saundersfoot,
where the wagons, originally horse drawn
but eventually pulled by steam trains,
ran along the main street. Although the
tracks have long gone, you can still follow
its course along the Miners' Walk past
Coppett Hall into the town, going through
three tunnels along the way.

3. At the far end of the beach, double
back right on a narrow lane above the
stream into **Pleasant Valley**. At a fork by
a **cottage**, bear off along a quiet track
that follows the line of an **old tramway**,
ultimately coming out onto another
lane by the entrance to **Heritage Park**,

Sandy shore: *Amroth beach is half a mile long with a huge expanse of sand at low tide*

a lodge development on the site of a former iron works.

4. Cross the lane to **Mill House Caravan Park** opposite. Follow the drive ahead, but as it then bends, walk forward to a stile behind the caravans. Bear left up a hillside grazing to a gap in the top wall and cross out onto a narrow lane. Go right over a rise, dropping to a sharp bend beyond.

5. Keep ahead along a drive, leaving that where it then forks for a footpath signed off over a stile on the right. Climb away

to the left across the slope of an open-wooded hill, ignoring crosspaths to find a stile at the top. Follow the left field edge to reach a track and go briefly rig as far as a bend. Turn off left through a kissing gate along a wooded path that leads to **Cwmrath Farm.**

6. Joining its access track, walk out to a lane. Turn right, crossing to then leave almost immediately along another farr track on the left. Entering the **yard**, keep ahead along a waymarked path that heads down into a **wooded valle** Keep with it, winding downhill to a junction of tracks at the bottom. Walk forward past a small building, crossing

...idge over a stream and rising beyond ...to a lane. Turn right up the hill, ...ssing the private entrance to **Colby** ...dge. Take the next right into **Colby** ...odland Gardens, where you will ...d the **Bothy Tearoom**.

7. To return to **Amroth**, continue beyond the tearoom, following the drive on down the valley. Eventually passing **cottages**, keep going to join a lane, which leads down back to the **car park**, to complete the walk. ♦

Fossilised forest

After the last Ice Age, sea levels were lower than today, and woodland extended far into the bay at Amroth, where early man hunted and foraged as he moved along the coast. Walk out at extreme low tide and you will discover the blackened remains of petrified tree stumps. Look closely and you may also come across fossilised hazelnuts, fragments of horn and bone or even worked flint used as arrowheads.

Useful Information

Visit Pembrokeshire
Pembrokeshire's official tourism website covers everything from accommodation and special events to attractions and adventure. **www.visitpembrokeshire.com**

Pembrokeshire Coast National Park
The Pembrokeshire Coast National Park website also has information on things to see and do, plus a host of practical details to help plan your visit.

www.pembrokeshirecoast.org.uk

Tourist Information Centres
The main TICs provide free information on everything from accommodation and travel to what's on and walking advice.

St David's	01437 720392 | info@orielyparc.co.uk
Milford Haven	01437 771818 | milford.tic@pembrokeshire.gov.uk
Pembroke	01437 776499 | pembroke.tic@pembrokeshire.gov.uk
Tenby	01834 845040 | tenbycentre@pembrokeshirecoast.org.uk
Tenby	01834 842404 | tenby.tic@pembrokeshire.gov.uk
Saundersfoot	01834 813672 | saundersfoot.tic@pembrokeshire.gov.uk

Travel
Main **railway stations** are located at Tenby, Pembroke and Pembroke Dock. Information is available from National Rail Enquiries on 08457 484950 or **www.nationalrail.com.uk**. A dedicated **bus network** serves the whole of the Coast Path, running every day during the summer months but with a limited service in winter. Pembrokeshire Greenways - 01437 776313 - **www.pembrokeshiregreenways.co.uk** Traveline Cymru - 0871 200 22 33 - **www.travelinecymru.info**

Weather
The Met Office operates a 24 hour online weather forecast for Pembrokeshire. See **www.metoffice.gov.uk**